SH❛C
PRAYERS
TO CHANGE
YOUR
LIFE

HARVEST HOUSE PUBLISHERS
EUGENE, OREGON

Short Prayers to Change Your Life
Copyright © 2020 by PLJ Communications
Published by Harvest House Publishers
Eugene, Oregon 97408
www.harvesthousepublishers.com

ISBN 978-0-7369-7924-5 (pbk)
ISBN 978-0-7369-7925-2 (eBook)

Design by Peter Gloege | LOOK Design Studio

Printed in the United States of America
20 21 22 23 24 25 26 27 28 / VP / 10 9 8 7 6 5 4 3 2 1

CONTENTS

EVERYTHING STARTS FROM PRAYER.

WITHOUT ASKING GOD
FOR LOVE, WE CANNOT
POSSESS LOVE
AND STILL LESS ARE
WE ABLE TO GIVE IT
TO OTHERS.

—MOTHER TERESA

SEEK

PRAY, AND
LET GOD WORRY.

—MARTIN LUTHER

O GOD, EARLY IN THE MORNING
I CRY TO YOU.
HELP ME TO PRAY AND TO
CONCENTRATE MY THOUGHTS ON YOU;
I CANNOT DO THIS ALONE.

—DIETRICH BONHOEFFER

THE LORD HAS HEARD
MY PLEA FOR HELP;
THE LORD ACCEPTS
MY PRAYER.

—PSALM 6:9 HCSB

GOD GRANT ME

THE **SERENITY**

TO ACCEPT THE THINGS

I CANNOT CHANGE,

COURAGE TO CHANGE

THE THINGS I CAN,

AND **WISDOM** TO KNOW

THE DIFFERENCE.

—REINHOLD NIEBUHR

IS ANYONE AMONG YOU IN TROUBLE?

THEN THAT PERSON SHOULD PRAY.

—JAMES 5:13 NIRV

———

WHEN **I PRAY,**
COINCIDENCES HAPPEN,
AND WHEN I DON'T,
THEY DON'T.

—WILLIAM TEMPLE

OH, LORD! YOU'VE BEEN WITH ME IN SIX TROUBLES.

DON'T DESERT ME IN THE SEVENTH!

—HARRIET TUBMAN

DEAR GOD,
I HAVE SO MANY
BURDENS
TODAY.

MAY I
LEAVE THEM
WITH
YOU?

TRUE PRAYERS
ARE LIKE THOSE
CARRIER PIGEONS WHICH
FIND THEIR WAY SO WELL;
THEY CANNOT FAIL
TO GO TO HEAVEN,
FOR IT IS FROM HEAVEN
THAT THEY CAME;
THEY ARE ONLY GOING HOME.

—CHARLES SPURGEON

O, GOD,

I ASK FOR **LOVE AND LIGHT**

FOR THOSE LIVING IN DARKNESS

AND **HEALING RELIEF**

FOR ALL WHO ARE HURTING.

⚜

**HE HEALS THE BROKENHEARTED
AND BINDS UP THEIR WOUNDS.**

—PSALM 147:3

GOD,

I AM TRYING TO

RECOVER MY FAITH.

PLEASE DON'T

ABANDON ME

IN THE MIDDLE OF

THIS ADVENTURE.

—PAULO COELHO

BEHOLD, LORD...

I AM WEAK IN FAITH;

STRENGTHEN THOU ME.

I AM COLD IN LOVE;

WARM ME AND

MAKE ME FERVENT

THAT MY LOVE

MAY GO OUT

TO MY NEIGHBOR.

—MARTIN LUTHER

DEAR LORD,
PLEASE RESTORE
MY PATIENCE.
MINE IS ALMOST
GONE. AMEN.

———

IN PRAYER IT IS BETTER

TO HAVE A HEART WITHOUT WORDS

THAN WORDS WITHOUT A HEART.

—JOHN BUNYAN

DEAR LORD, PLEASE GUARD

MY

TODAY, FOR EVERYTHING I DO FLOWS FROM IT.

MAY GOD BREAK MY HEART
SO COMPLETELY THAT
THE WHOLE WORLD FALLS IN.

—MOTHER TERESA

COME, LORD, SET US ON FIRE.

CLASP US CLOSE TO YOUR BOSOM.

SEDUCE US WITH YOUR BEAUTY.

ENCHANT US WITH YOUR FRAGRANCE.

LET US LOVE YOU.

—SAINT AUGUSTINE

MAY PEACE
REIGN OVER EARTH,
MAY THE GOURD CUP
AGREE WITH [THE] VESSEL.
PEACE BE WITH US.

—KENYAN BLESSING

GO **WHERE** YOUR
BEST PRAYERS TAKE YOU.

—FREDERICK BUECHNER

GOD...

SAVE US

≫→ FROM ←≪

DECEIVING OURSELVES

BY PRIDE OR VANITY.

—JANE AUSTEN

LOVING GOD OF EACH NEW DAY,

TODAY
MAY I CHOOSE MY
WORDS WITH CARE,

TODAY
MAY I LIFT THE SPIRITS
OF ANY WHO STRUGGLE,

TODAY
MAY I BE WILLING TO FORGIVE,
AND TO SEEK FORGIVENESS,

TODAY
MAY I LOVE OTHERS,
AS YOU HAVE LOVED ME.

AMEN.

LORD JESUS CHRIST, MAY I

DREAM OF YOUR SWEETNESS,

REST IN YOUR ARMS,

BE AT ONE WITH YOUR FATHER,

AND BE COMFORTED

IN THE KNOWLEDGE THAT YOU

ALWAYS WATCH OVER ME.

—ERASMUS

IF
I CAN DO
NOTHING ELSE,
I WILL PRAY.

—MARIANNE
ADLARD

LORD, HELP ME
NOT TO DESPISE OR OPPOSE
WHAT I DO
NOT UNDERSTAND.

—WILLIAM PENN

———

THE LORD IS WATCHING
HIS CHILDREN,
LISTENING TO THEIR PRAYERS.

—1 PETER 3:12 TLB

HEAVENLY FATHER,

WHO MAKES US ONE,

MAY WE BE YOUR CHILDREN WHO

ENCOURAGE EACH OTHER,

LISTEN TO EACH OTHER,

LEARN FROM EACH OTHER,

SPEAK THE TRUTH TO EACH OTHER,

FORGIVE EACH OTHER, AND

LOVE EACH OTHER.

AMEN.

> DEAR GOD,
> IF SOMETHING
> BREAKS YOUR HEART,
> MAY IT BREAK MINE
> AS WELL.

NEVER
STOP PRAYING.

—1 THESSALONIANS 5:17 NLT

GOOD MORNING, GOD!

WHAT DO YOU HAVE
IN STORE FOR ME TODAY?

·········· ❧ ··········

I HAVE SO MUCH TO DO
THAT I SHALL SPEND
THE FIRST THREE HOURS
IN PRAYER.

—MARTIN LUTHER

FATHER GOD,

I AM TIRED AND BROKEN.

I WANT TO REST

IN YOUR ARMS.

CAST YOUR CARES ON THE LORD
AND HE WILL SUSTAIN YOU;
HE WILL NEVER LET THE RIGHTEOUS
BE SHAKEN.

—PSALM 55:22

O LORD,

MY HEART IS ALL A PRAYER,

BUT IT IS SILENT UNTO THEE;

I AM TOO TIRED

TO LOOK FOR WORDS,

I REST UPON THY SYMPATHY.

—AMY CARMICHAEL

LET MY HEART
KNOW YOUR PEACE,
O GOD.

TAKE DELIGHT IN THE LORD,

AND HE WILL GIVE YOU

THE DESIRES OF YOUR HEART.

—PSALM 37:4

JESUS, NOURISHING BREAD OF LIFE,

JESUS, REFRESHING WATER OF LIFE,

JESUS, LORD OF ALL LIFE, BE WITH ME.

JESUS, LORD OF LOVE,

HOLD ME, YOUR CHILD,

CLOSE TO YOUR HEART.

—INSPIRED BY AN AFRICAN BLESSING

HERE, LORD,
IS MY LIFE.
I PLACE IT ON THE
ALTAR TODAY.
USE IT AS YOU WILL.

—ALBERT SCHWEITZER

———

THE DEVIL...
TREMBLES WHEN WE PRAY.

—SAMUEL CHADWICK

MAY JESUS BE IN EVERY EYE THAT SEES ME AND IN EVERY EAR THAT HEARS ME.

—INSPIRED BY A PRAYER
OF SAINT PATRICK

TO PRAY IS TO DREAM
IN LEAGUE WITH GOD,
TO ENVISION
HIS HOLY VISIONS.

—ABRAHAM HESCHEL

MAY I
GIVE THANKS TO YOU
THROUGH GENEROSITY
AND KINDNESS
TO ALL YOUR CHILDREN.
AMEN.

ANY CONCERN TOO SMALL
TO BE TURNED INTO A PRAYER
IS TOO SMALL
TO BE MADE INTO A BURDEN.

—CORRIE TEN BOOM

SPEAK, LORD, FOR YOUR SERVANT IS LISTENING.

PRAYER IS
KEEPING COMPANY
WITH GOD.

—CLEMENT OF ALEXANDRIA

TEACH ME, LORD,

TO SING OF YOUR MERCIES.

TURN MY SOUL INTO A GARDEN,

WHERE THE FLOWERS DANCE

IN THE GARDEN BREEZE,

PRAISING YOU WITH

THEIR BEAUTY.

—TERESA OF AVILA

LORD,
WORK WONDERS
IN ME, AND FOR ME.

—CHARLES SPURGEON

❧

PRAYER IS NOT JUST ASKING.

IT IS LISTENING

FOR GOD'S ORDERS.

—BILLY GRAHAM

DEAR LORD,
MORE OF YOU,
LESS OF ME.

———

PRAYER DOES NOT FIT US
FOR GREATER WORK;
PRAYER *IS* THE GREATER WORK.

—OSWALD CHAMBERS

CREATE IN ME A

CLEAN HEART, O GOD,

AND RENEW A RIGHT SPIRIT

WITHIN ME.

—KING DAVID
PSALM 51:10 ESV

PRAYER DOES NOT
CHANGE GOD,
BUT IT CHANGES HIM
WHO PRAYS.

—SOREN KIERKEGAARD

LORD,
HAVE MERCY.

❧

OUR PRAYERS MAY BE AWKWARD.

OUR ATTEMPTS MAY BE FEEBLE.

BUT SINCE THE POWER OF PRAYER

IS IN THE ONE WHO HEARS IT AND NOT

IN THE ONE WHO SAYS IT, OUR PRAYERS DO

MAKE A DIFFERENCE.

— MAX LUCADO

A BLESSING OF
SAINT IGNATIUS*

LORD JESUS, TEACH US TO BE GENEROUS;

TEACH US TO SERVE YOU AS YOU DESERVE,

TO GIVE AND NOT TO COUNT THE COST,

TO FIGHT AND NOT TO HEED THE WOUNDS,

TO TOIL AND NOT TO SEEK FOR REST,

TO LABOUR AND NOT TO SEEK REWARD,

EXCEPT THAT OF KNOWING THAT

WE DO YOUR WILL.

* Saint Ignatius of Loyola was a sixteenth-century Spanish knight who dedicated his life to Jesus after being seriously wounded in battle. He was a fierce man of prayer, often spending seven hours a day communing with his Lord Jesus.

LORD,
MAKE ME SEE THY
GLORY IN
EVERY PLACE.

—MICHELANGELO

THIS IS THE CONFIDENCE WE HAVE
IN APPROACHING GOD:
THAT IF WE ASK ANYTHING
ACCORDING TO HIS WILL, HE HEARS US.

—1 JOHN 5:14

FORGIVE ME MY NONSENSE AS I
ALSO FORGIVE THE NONSENSE
OF THOSE WHO THINK
THEY TALK SENSE.

—ROBERT FROST

———

PRAYER IS NOT ASKING.
PRAYER IS PUTTING ONESELF IN
THE HANDS OF GOD,
AT HIS DISPOSITION, AND
LISTENING TO HIS VOICE
IN THE DEPTH OF OUR HEARTS.

—MOTHER TERESA

MY FATHER, IF IT IS POSSIBLE,

MAY THIS CUP BE TAKEN FROM ME.

YET NOT AS I WILL, BUT AS YOU WILL.

—JESUS CHRIST
MATTHEW 26:39

I HAVE BEEN DRIVEN MANY TIMES

UPON MY KNEES

BY THE OVERWHELMING CONVICTION

THAT I HAD NOWHERE ELSE TO GO.

MY OWN WISDOM

AND THAT OF ALL ABOUT ME SEEMED

INSUFFICIENT FOR THAT DAY.

—ABRAHAM LINCOLN

I TRUST YOU ALWAYS THOUGH
I MAY SEEM TO BE LOST AND
IN THE SHADOW OF DEATH.
I WILL NOT FEAR, FOR YOU
ARE EVER WITH ME, AND YOU WILL NEVER
LEAVE ME TO FACE MY PERILS ALONE.

—THOMAS MERTON

THE LORD IS CLOSE
TO THE BROKENHEARTED,
AND HE SAVES THOSE
WHOSE SPIRITS
HAVE BEEN CRUSHED.

—PSALM 34:18 NCV

I DO BELIEVE;
HELP ME OVERCOME
MY UNBELIEF!

—MARK 9:24

GOD DOES NOTHING BUT IN ANSWER
TO PRAYER...EVERY NEW VICTORY
WHICH A SOUL GAINS IS THE EFFECT
OF A NEW PRAYER.

—JOHN WESLEY

I'M GOING TO HOLD STEADY ON TO YOU, AND I KNOW YOU WILL SEE ME THROUGH.

—HARRIET TUBMAN*

*   This prayer was recited regularly by Harriet Tubman when she led runaway
    slaves to freedom in the northern United States via the Underground Railroad.

WE BESEECH YOU, MASTER,
TO BE OUR HELPER AND PROTECTOR.
SAVE THE AFFLICTED AMONG US;
HAVE MERCY ON THE LOWLY;
RAISE UP THE FALLEN.

—SAINT CLEMENT OF ROME

IS **PRAYER**
YOUR STEERING WHEEL OR
YOUR SPARE TIRE?

—CORRIE TEN BOOM

SHOW ME
THE WAY, LORD.

PRAYER SHOULD NOT BE REGARDED
AS A DUTY WHICH MUST BE
PERFORMED, BUT RATHER AS A
PRIVILEGE TO BE ENJOYED,
A RARE DELIGHT THAT IS ALWAYS
REVEALING SOME NEW BEAUTY.

—E.M. BOUNDS

PRAISE

GIVE US GRACE,
ALMIGHTY FATHER,
SO TO PRAY, AS TO
DESERVE TO BE HEARD,
TO ADDRESS THEE
WITH OUR HEARTS,
AS WITH OUR LIPS.

—JANE AUSTEN

DEAR LORD,
I PRAISE YOU TODAY
FOR YOUR GOODNESS
TOMORROW.

PRAY FOR PRAYER.

PRAY UNTIL YOU CAN REALLY PRAY.

—CHARLES SPURGEON

MY HEART IS

THANKFUL

FOR YOUR WONDERS,
MY MARVELOUS
CREATOR.

SING A NEW SONG
TO THE **LORD**,
FOR HE HAS DONE
WONDERFUL DEEDS.

—PSALM 98:1 NLT

I LOVE YOU, LORD.

YOU ARE MY STRENGTH.

YOU ARE MY ROCK,

MY PROTECTION, MY SAVIOR.

I CAN RUN TO YOU

FOR SAFETY.

YOU ARE MY SHIELD,

MY SAVING STRENGTH,

AND MY DEFENDER.

—INSPIRED BY PSALM 18:2

I ARISE TODAY

THROUGH THE MIGHTY STRENGTH

OF THE LORD OF CREATION.

I ARISE TODAY

THROUGH THE STRENGTH OF HEAVEN;

LIGHT OF THE SUN,

SPLENDOR OF FIRE,

SPEED OF LIGHTNING,

SWIFTNESS OF THE WIND,

DEPTH OF THE SEA.

—SAINT PATRICK

IN THE MORNING, LORD, YOU HEAR MY VOICE;

IN THE MORNING I LAY MY REQUESTS BEFORE YOU

AND WAIT EXPECTANTLY.

FOR YOU ARE NOT A GOD WHO IS PLEASED

WITH WICKEDNESS;

WITH YOU, EVIL PEOPLE ARE NOT WELCOME...

BUT I, BY YOUR GREAT LOVE,

CAN COME INTO YOUR HOUSE;

IN REVERENCE I BOW DOWN.

—PSALM 5:3-4,7

GOOD NIGHT! GOOD NIGHT!

FAR FLIES THE LIGHT;

BUT STILL GOD'S LOVE

SHALL SHINE ABOVE,

MAKING ALL BRIGHT,

GOOD NIGHT! GOOD NIGHT!

—VICTOR HUGO

YOU ARE HOLY, LORD,
THE ONLY GOD,
AND YOUR DEEDS ARE WONDERFUL.
YOU ARE STRONG.
YOU ARE GREAT.
YOU ARE THE MOST HIGH.
YOU ARE ALMIGHTY.

—SAINT FRANCIS OF ASSISI

GIVE THANKS TO THE LORD,
FOR HE IS GOOD!
HIS FAITHFUL LOVE
ENDURES FOREVER.

—PSALM 107:1 NLT

THIS DAY IS A GIFT

I UNWRAP WITH

GRATITUDE

AND JOY.

I THANK AND

WORSHIP YOU, GOD!

LORD JESUS,

LET ME KNOW MYSELF AND KNOW THEE...

LET ME DO EVERYTHING FOR THE SAKE OF THEE.

LET ME HUMBLE MYSELF AND EXALT THEE.

—SAINT AUGUSTINE

———

TRUE PRAYER IS NEITHER A MERE
MENTAL EXERCISE NOR A VOCAL PERFORMANCE.
IT IS FAR DEEPER THAN THAT—
IT IS SPIRITUAL TRANSACTION WITH
THE CREATOR OF HEAVEN AND EARTH.

—CHARLES SPURGEON

JESUS, IN YOU ALONE MY SOUL FINDS REST. AMEN.

WHEN
WE COME TO
THE END OF OURSELVES,
WE COME TO
THE BEGINNING OF GOD.

—BILLY GRAHAM

NOW TO HIM WHO CAN KEEP YOU
ON YOUR FEET, STANDING TALL
IN HIS BRIGHT PRESENCE,
FRESH AND CELEBRATING—

TO OUR ONE GOD,

OUR ONLY SAVIOR...JESUS CHRIST,
OUR MASTER,
BE GLORY, MAJESTY,
STRENGTH, AND RULE...
NOW, AND TO THE END
OF ALL TIME. YES!

—JUDE 24-25 MSG

BLESSED ART THOU,

O LORD OUR GOD,

KING OF THE UNIVERSE,

WHO GIVEST STRENGTH

TO THE WEARY.

—HEBREW PRAYER

TIME SPENT IN
PRAYER
IS NEVER
WASTED.

—FRANCIS FENELON

O HEAVENLY FATHER,

WHO HAST FILLED THE WORLD WITH BEAUTY:
OPEN OUR EYES TO BEHOLD
THY GRACIOUS HAND IN ALL THY WORKS;

THAT, REJOICING IN THY
WHOLE CREATION, WE MAY LEARN
TO SERVE THEE WITH GLADNESS;

FOR THE SAKE OF HIM THROUGH
WHOM ALL THINGS WERE MADE,
THY SON JESUS CHRIST, OUR LORD. AMEN.

—THE BOOK OF COMMON PRAYER

GUIDE MY GOING IN
AND GOING FORWARD,
AND LEAD HOME MY GOING FORTH.
YOU ARE TRUE GOD AND TRUE MAN,
AND LIVE FOR EVER AND EVER.

—SAINT THOMAS AQUINAS

NO MAN IS GREATER
THAN HIS PRAYER LIFE.

—LEONARD RAVENHILL

GLORY BE TO THE FATHER,

AND TO THE SON,

AND TO THE HOLY SPIRIT.

AS IT WAS IN THE BEGINNING,

IS NOW, AND EVER SHALL BE,

WORLD WITHOUT END.

AMEN.

—THE LESSER DOXOLOGY

LORD, MAY I

HONOR YOU TODAY

BY SLOWING DOWN,

OPENING MY EYES,

AND APPRECIATING THE BEAUTY

ALL AROUND ME.

PRAYER SHOULD BE
THE KEY OF THE DAY AND
THE LOCK OF THE NIGHT.

—GEORGE HERBERT

LOVING CREATOR,

I PRAISE YOU FOR MAKING ME A UNIQUE

REFLECTION OF YOUR IMAGE.

I ASK YOU, HUMBLY...

OPEN MY EYES TO YOUR WONDERS.

OPEN MY MIND TO YOUR TRUTHS.

OPEN MY LIFE TO YOUR PURPOSE.

OPEN MY HEART TO RECEIVE YOUR LOVE—

AND TO SHARE IT

EVERY DAY.

AMEN.

ALL THINGS LIVE IN YOU, O GOD.

YOU COMMAND US TO SEEK YOU,

AND YOU ARE ALWAYS READY TO BE FOUND.

TO KNOW YOU IS LIFE,
TO SERVE YOU IS FREEDOM,
TO PRAISE YOU IS JOY.

WE BLESS AND ADORE YOU,

WORSHIP AND MAGNIFY YOU,

THANK AND LOVE YOU.

—SAINT AUGUSTINE

NOW TO HIM WHO IS ABLE
TO DO IMMEASURABLY MORE THAN ALL
WE ASK OR IMAGINE, ACCORDING TO
HIS POWER THAT IS AT WORK WITHIN US,
TO HIM BE GLORY IN THE CHURCH AND IN
CHRIST JESUS THROUGHOUT ALL GENERATIONS,
FOR EVER AND EVER! AMEN.

—EPHESIANS 3:20-21

WHEN YOU FEEL LIKE WORRYING,
TRY PRAYING INSTEAD.
WORRYING ONLY CREATES MORE
STRESS, BUT PRAYER CREATES
MORE PEACE.

—DAVE WILLIS

O, GOD, I THANK THEE

FOR SUCH DIRECT MANIFESTATION OF THY GOODNESS, MAJESTY, AND POWER!

—GEORGE WASHINGTON CARVER,
"UPON SEEING A SUNSET"

BLESSINGS ARE MORE CHERISHED BY THOSE WHO BEAR THE SPIRIT OF GRATITUDE.

—EDMOND MBIAKA

WONDERFUL GOD OF PROMISES,
ALL MY LIFE, YOUR HAND HAS LED ME,
I KNOW YOU ARE WITH ME EVERYWHERE.
YOU HAVE WARMED AND CLOTHED
AND FED ME. SO I PRAISE YOU
NOW IN PRAYER.

———

YOU ARE GOD-ENTHRONED,
SURROUNDED WITH SONGS,
LIVING AMONG THE SHOUTS OF PRAISE
OF YOUR PRINCELY PEOPLE.

—PSALM 22:3 TPT

DEAR GOD,

YOU ARE AWESOME.

THAT IS ALL.

❧

IF YOU BELIEVE IN PRAYER AT ALL,
EXPECT GOD TO HEAR YOU.

— CHARLES SPURGEON

PRAYER OF
SAINT RICHARD*

THANKS BE TO THEE,

MY LORD JESUS CHRIST,

FOR ALL THE BENEFITS

THOU HAST GIVEN ME,

FOR ALL THE PAINS AND INSULTS

THOU HAST BORNE FOR ME.

O MOST MERCIFUL REDEEMER,

FRIEND AND BROTHER,

MAY I KNOW THEE MORE CLEARLY,

LOVE THEE MORE DEARLY,

AND FOLLOW THEE MORE NEARLY,

DAY BY DAY. AMEN.

*   This prayer, dating to the thirteenth century, is said to have been uttered by
    Saint Richard, the Bishop of Chichester (1197-1253), hours before his death.

DON'T PRAY

WHEN IT RAINS

IF YOU

DON'T PRAY

WHEN THE

SUN SHINES.

—SATCHEL PAIGE

HOLY, HOLY, HOLY IS
the LORD ALMIGHTY;
THE WHOLE EARTH IS FULL
of HIS GLORY.

—THE SERAPHIM
ISAIAH 6:3

MOST-KIND GOD,

YOU HAVE DONE GREAT THINGS FOR ME,

AND I AM FILLED WITH JOY!

—INSPIRED BY PSALM 126:3

❦

PRAYER IS THE CONTACT
OF A LIVING SOUL WITH GOD.
IN PRAYER, GOD STOOPS TO KISS MAN,
TO BLESS MAN, AND TO AID IN
EVERYTHING THAT GOD CAN DEVISE
OR MAN CAN NEED.

—E.M. BOUNDS

PRAISE BE TO THE GOD

AND FATHER OF OUR

LORD JESUS CHRIST,

WHO HAS BLESSED US

IN THE HEAVENLY REALMS

WITH EVERY SPIRITUAL

BLESSING IN CHRIST.

—EPHESIANS 1:3

I PRAISE YOU, LORD, FOR
RESTORING
MY SOUL.

—INSPIRED BY PSALM 23:3

———

I HOPE I AM
PROPERLY GRATEFUL
TO THE ALMIGHTY
FOR HAVING BEEN SO
WELL SUPPORTED.

—JANE AUSTEN

HOSANNA TO GOD,
WHO REIGNS WITH LOVE!

WE DO NOT THINK OURSELVES
INTO NEW WAYS OF LIVING.
WE LIVE OURSELVES
INTO NEW WAYS OF THINKING.

—RICHARD ROHR

WHEN I SEE THE MOON

IN THE NIGHT SKY,

I SPEAK MY

EVENING PRAYER:

PRAISE BE TO

THE BEING OF LIFE,

FOR HIS KINDNESS

AND HIS GOODNESS.

—ANCIENT CELTIC PRAYER

HEAVENLY FATHER,

I PRAISE YOU BECAUSE

YOUR **LOVE** FOR ME

IS MIGHTIER THAN THE

WAVES OF THE SEA.

—INSPIRED BY PSALM 93:4

ALL THINGS MUST COME
TO THE SOUL FROM ITS ROOTS,
FROM WHERE IT IS PLANTED.

—SAINT TERESA OF AVILA

OPEN WIDE THE WINDOW

OF OUR SPIRITS, O LORD,

AND FILL US FULL OF LIGHT;

OPEN WIDE THE DOOR
OF OUR HEARTS,

THAT WE MAY RECEIVE

AND ENTERTAIN THEE

WITH ALL OUR POWERS OF

ADORATION AND LOVE.

—CHRISTINA ROSETTI

FATHER GOD,

WE PRAISE YOU FOR THE WONDERFUL
FUTURE THAT YOU HAVE PREPARED
FOR US THROUGH THE DEATH AND
RESURRECTION OF YOUR SON, JESUS.
AMEN.

———

YOU CAN DO MORE THAN PRAY,
AFTER YOU HAVE PRAYED,
BUT YOU CANNOT DO MORE THAN
PRAY *UNTIL* YOU HAVE PRAYED.

—JOHN BUNYAN

LOOK UPON US,

O LORD,

AND LET ALL

THE DARKNESS

OF OUR SOULS

VANISH BEFORE

THE BEAMS OF THY

BRIGHTNESS.

—SAINT AUGUSTINE

L

GOD

O

V

E

LATE IN HIS LIFE, IN A CHRISTMAS CARD
TO HIS FRIENDS, MUSICIAN AND COMPOSER
DUKE ELLINGTON CREATED
THIS PRAYER AS HIS WAY TO CONVEY
GOD'S LOVE FOR HUMANITY.

BE JOYFUL IN HOPE,
PATIENT IN AFFLICTION,
FAITHFUL IN PRAYER.

—ROMANS 12:12

IN THE SILENCE OF THE HEART

GOD SPEAKS.

IF YOU FACE GOD IN PRAYER AND SILENCE,

GOD WILL SPEAK TO YOU.

—MOTHER TERESA

———

I WILL SAY OF THE LORD,

"HE IS MY REFUGE AND MY FORTRESS,

MY GOD, IN WHOM I TRUST."

—KING DAVID
PSALM 91:2

ETERNAL AND EVERLASTING GOD,
WHO ART THE FATHER OF ALL MANKIND,
AS WE TURN ASIDE FROM THE HURLY-BURLY
OF EVERYDAY LIVING, MAY OUR
HEARTS AND SOULS, YEA OUR VERY SPIRITS,
BE LIFTED UPWARD TO THEE.

—CORETTA SCOTT KING

ABOVE ALL, PUT ON LOVE—
THE PERFECT BOND OF UNITY.

—COLOSSIANS 3:14 HCSB

I PRAISE YOU

FOR ALL THINGS,

I BLESS YOU,

I GLORIFY YOU

THROUGH THE ETERNAL PRIEST

OF HEAVEN, JESUS CHRIST,

YOUR BELOVED SON.

THROUGH HIM BE GLORY TO YOU,

TOGETHER WITH HIM

AND THE HOLY SPIRIT,

NOW AND FOR EVER. AMEN.

—POLYCARP

WE ACKNOWLEDGE THEE,

THE ONLY GOD.

WE OWN THEE AS OUR KING.

—CONSTANTINE

TRUST IN THE LORD
WITH ALL YOUR HEART,
AND DO NOT RELY ON
YOUR OWN UNDERSTANDING;
THINK ABOUT HIM IN ALL YOUR WAYS,
AND HE WILL GUIDE YOU
ON THE RIGHT PATHS.

—PROVERBS 3:5-6 HCSB

I PRAISE YOU BECAUSE I AM FEARFULLY
AND WONDERFULLY MADE;
YOUR WORKS ARE WONDERFUL,
I KNOW THAT FULL WELL.

—PSALM 139:14

———

THE LORD STANDS ABOVE
THE NEW DAY,
FOR GOD HAS MADE IT.
ALL RESTLESSNESS,
ALL WORRY, AND ANXIETY
FLEE BEFORE HIM.

—DIETRICH BONHOEFFER

BLESS

GOD BESTOWS
HIS BLESSINGS
WITHOUT
DISCRIMINATION.

—F.F. BRUCE

DEEP PEACE
OF THE RUNNING WAVES TO YOU,

DEEP PEACE
OF THE FLOWING AIR TO YOU,

DEEP PEACE
OF THE QUIET EARTH TO YOU,

DEEP PEACE OF THE
SHINING STARS TO YOU.

DEEP PEACE OF THE
SHADES OF NIGHT TO YOU,

MOON AND STARS
ALWAYS GIVING LIGHT TO YOU,

DEEP PEACE OF CHRIST,
THE SON OF PEACE, TO YOU.

—TRADITIONAL GAELIC BLESSING

MAY YOU LIVE A LIFE
WORTHY OF OUR LORD.

MAY YOU PLEASE HIM IN EVERY WAY,

AS YOU DO GOOD THINGS AND
LEARN MORE AND MORE

ABOUT GOD AND HIS AMAZING SON.

MAY HE GIVE YOU STRENGTH
AND ENDURANCE.

MAY YOU GIVE JOYFUL THANKS
ALWAYS TO THE ONE

WHO HAS LET YOU ENTER
THE KINGDOM OF LIGHT.

—BASED ON COLOSSIANS 1:9-12

WHEN AT NIGHT I GO TO SLEEP,

FOURTEEN ANGELS WATCH DO KEEP,

TWO MY HEAD ARE GUARDING,

TWO MY FEET ARE GUIDING;

TWO UPON MY RIGHT HAND,

TWO UPON MY LEFT HAND.

TWO WHO WARMLY COVER,

TWO WHO O'ER ME HOVER,

TWO TO WHOM 'TIS GIVEN

TO GUIDE MY STEPS TO HEAVEN.

—GERMAN BLESSING

MAY GOD BLESS YOU TODAY
AND EVERY DAY IN THE FUTURE.
MAY YOU HEAR HIS VOICE,
FEEL HIS LOVE,
AND FOLLOW HIS PATH.
MAY YOU LIVE FOREVER
IN HIS GRACE.

AMEN.

> WOULD THAT CHRIST
> WOULD TEACH MY SOUL
> A PRAYER THAT WOULD PLEAD
> TO THE FATHER FOR GRACE
> SUFFICIENT FOR YOU.
>
> —CLARA BARTON

IF **GOD** SENDS YOU
DOWN A STONY PATH,
MAY HE GIVE YOU
STRONG SHOES.

—TRADITIONAL CELTIC BLESSING

❧

LOVE THE PEOPLE WHO
TREAT YOU RIGHT,
PRAY FOR THE ONES WHO DO NOT.
LIFE IS TOO SHORT TO BE
ANYTHING BUT HAPPY.
FALLING DOWN IS A PART OF LIFE,
GETTING BACK UP IS LIVING.

—JOSÉ N. HARRIS

MAY THE LORD

MAKE YOU HOLY.

MAY HIS BLESSINGS SPRINKLE

GENTLY ON YOU

LIKE REFRESHING SPRING RAIN.

—INSPIRED BY DEUTERONOMY 28:12

A GENEROUS PERSON

WILL BE BLESSED.

—PROVERBS 22:9 HCSB

MAY THE BLESSING

OF LIGHT BE ON YOU—

LIGHT WITHOUT AND

LIGHT WITHIN.

MAY THE BLESSED SUNLIGHT

SHINE ON YOU

LIKE A GREAT PEAT FIRE,

SO THAT STRANGER AND FRIEND

MAY COME AND

WARM HIMSELF AT IT.

—SCOTTISH BLESSING

MAY THE LORD YOUR GOD
LIFT YOU HIGH.

MAY YOU BE BLESSED
IN THE BIG, BUSY CITY OR THE
QUIET SMALL TOWN.

MAY GOD BLESS THE WORK
OF YOUR HANDS AND YOUR BRAIN.

MAY YOU BE BLESSED
IN YOUR HOME, AND FAR,
FAR BEYOND YOUR HOME.

—INSPIRED BY DEUTERONOMY 28:1-12

MAY OUR GOD BLESS YOU
AND TAKE GOOD CARE OF YOU.

MAY HE BE KIND TO YOU
AND DO GOOD THINGS FOR YOU.

MAY HE SMILE LOVINGLY
WHENEVER HE LOOKS AT YOU.

MAY HE HELP YOU FEEL
GOOD INSIDE AND GIVE YOU PEACE.

—INSPIRED BY NUMBERS 6:24-26

MAY THE GOD OF PEACE

BRING PEACE TO THIS HOUSE.

MAY THE SON OF PEACE

BRING PEACE TO THIS HOUSE.

MAY THE SPIRIT OF PEACE

BRING PEACE TO THIS HOUSE,

THIS NIGHT AND ALL NIGHTS.

—CELTIC PRAYER

O HEAVENLY FATHER,

PROTECT AND

BLESS ALL THINGS

THAT HAVE BREATH:

GUARD THEM

FROM ALL EVIL

AND LET THEM

SLEEP IN PEACE.

—ALBERT SCHWEITZER

IF THERE IS **RIGHTEOUSNESS** IN THE HEART,

THERE WILL BE **BEAUTY** IN THE CHARACTER.

IF THERE IS **BEAUTY** IN THE CHARACTER,

THERE WILL BE **HARMONY** IN THE HOME.

IF THERE IS **HARMONY** IN THE HOME,

THERE WILL BE **ORDER** IN THE NATION.

IF THERE IS **ORDER** IN THE NATION,

THERE WILL BE **PEACE** IN THE WORLD.

SO LET IT BE.

—SCOTTISH BLESSING

MAY THE TREASURE OF

GOD'S BLESSED LOVE

BE ALWAYS WITH YOU,

THE LOVE THAT SHINES

FROM THE OUTSIDE UPON YOU,

LIKE THE WARMING SUN,

AND THE LOVE THAT GLOWS

INSIDE YOUR PRECIOUS HEART,

LIKE A CANDLE WITH

AN EVERLASTING FLAME.

MAY THE SUN

BRING YOU NEW ENERGY BY DAY.

MAY THE MOON

SOFTLY RESTORE YOU BY NIGHT.

MAY THE RAIN

WASH AWAY YOUR WORRIES.

MAY THE BREEZE

BLOW NEW STRENGTH INTO
YOUR BEING.

MAY YOU WALK

GENTLY THROUGH THE WORLD
AND KNOW ITS BEAUTY ALL
THE DAYS OF YOUR LIFE.

—APACHE BLESSING

MAY GOD THE **FATHER** BLESS US,
MAY **CHRIST** TAKE CARE OF US,
THE **HOLY GHOST** ENLIGHTEN US
ALL THE DAYS OF OUR LIFE.
THE LORD BE OUR DEFENDER AND
KEEPER OF BODY AND SOUL,
BOTH NOW AND FOR EVER,
TO THE AGES OF AGES.

—SAINT ÆTHELWOLD

PRAY AT ALL TIMES IN THE SPIRIT
WITH EVERY PRAYER AND REQUEST,
AND STAY ALERT IN THIS
WITH ALL PERSEVERANCE.

—EPHESIANS 6:18 HCSB

BLESS THE FOUR CORNERS OF THIS HOUSE,

AND THE FOUNDATION BE BLESSED...

AND BLESS THE DOOR THAT OPENS WIDE,

TO OLD FRIENDS AND NEW.

AND BLESS THE ROOF OVER OUR HEADS

AND EVERY STURDY WALL—

THE PEACE OF HUMANKIND,

THE PEACE OF GOD,

THE PEACE OF YOUR LOVE ON US ALL.

—INSPIRED BY A TRADITIONAL CHRISTIAN BLESSING

MAY YOU ALWAYS HAVE

WALLS FOR THE WINDS,

A ROOF FOR THE RAIN,

A ROOF FOR THE RAIN,

TEA BESIDE THE FIRE,

LAUGHTER TO CHEER YOU,

THOSE YOU LOVE NEAR YOU,

AND ALL THAT YOUR HEART
MIGHT DESIRE.

—CELTIC BLESSING

WE RISE HIGHEST
WHEN WE LIFT OTHERS.

—TAYLOR MORGAN

O, YAHWEH,

BE TO ME, YOUR CHILD,

LIKE THE EVERGREEN TREE,

SHELTER ME IN YOUR SHADE.

PLEASE BLESS ME
AGAIN AND AGAIN,

LIKE THE WARM AND GENTLE RAIN,

THE RAIN THAT GIVES LIFE

TO ALL YOU HAVE MADE.

—INSPIRED BY THE BOOK OF HOSEA,
  (CHAPTERS 6 AND 14)

GOD BLESS US,
EVERY ONE!

—CHARLES DICKENS

❦

THOSE BLESSINGS ARE SWEETEST

THAT ARE **WON** WITH PRAYER

AND **WORN** WITH THANKS.

—THOMAS GOODWIN

MAY OUR LORD JESUS CHRIST HIMSELF
AND GOD OUR FATHER CHEER YOU ON
AND STRENGTHEN YOU IN EVERY
GOOD THING YOU DO AND SAY.

GOD LOVES YOU,

AND THROUGH HIS GRACE
HE GIVES YOU A GOOD HOPE
AND THE KIND OF HELP THAT GOES
ON FOREVER.

—INSPIRED BY
  2 THESSALONIANS 2:16-17

―――――――

SOMETIMES GOD MAKES BETTER CHOICES
FOR US THAN WE COULD HAVE EVER
MADE FOR OURSELVES.

—JENNIFER HUDSON TAYLOR

MAY WE ALL LIVE IN THE PEACE
THAT COMES FROM YOU.

MAY WE JOURNEY TOWARDS YOUR CITY,

SAILING THROUGH THE WATERS OF SIN

UNTOUCHED BY THE WAVES,

BORNE TRANQUILLY ALONG

BY THE HOLY SPIRIT.

—SAINT CLEMENT OF ALEXANDRIA
(AD 150 TO 215)

GOD IS ABLE TO BLESS YOU ABUNDANTLY,
SO THAT IN ALL THINGS AT ALL TIMES,
HAVING ALL THAT YOU NEED, YOU WILL
ABOUND IN EVERY GOOD WORK.

—2 CORINTHIANS 9:8

MAY THE
ALMIGHTY
SUSTAIN YOU ALL.

—JANE AUSTEN

PERHAPS ALL THE GOOD

THAT EVER HAS COME HERE

HAS COME BECAUSE PEOPLE

PRAYED IT INTO
THE WORLD.

—WENDELL BERRY

CHRIST WITH ME,
CHRIST BEFORE ME,
CHRIST BEHIND ME,

CHRIST IN ME,
CHRIST BENEATH ME,
CHRIST ABOVE ME,

CHRIST ON MY RIGHT,
CHRIST ON MY LEFT,
CHRIST WHERE I LIE,

CHRIST WHERE I SIT,
CHRIST WHERE I ARISE,
CHRIST IN THE HEART OF EVERYONE
WHO THINKS OF ME...

CHRIST IN EVERY EYE THAT SEES ME,
CHRIST IN EVERY EAR THAT HEARS ME,
SALVATION IS OF THE LORD.
SALVATION IS OF THE CHRIST.

MAY YOUR SALVATION, LORD,
BE EVER WITH US.

—SAINT PATRICK

YOU ARE WITH ME EVERYWHERE,
YOU PROMISE ME YOU'LL ALWAYS CARE.
KNOW ME, LEAD ME, LIGHT MY WAY
THROUGH EVERY HOUR OF EVERY DAY.
THROUGHOUT MY LIFE, IN ALL I DO,
KEEP ME ALWAYS CLOSE TO YOU.

—INSPIRED BY PSALM 139

———

IF YOU PRAY ONLY
WHEN YOU'RE IN TROUBLE,
THEN YOU *ARE* IN TROUBLE.

—TAYLOR MORGAN

GOD OF LOVE AND KINDNESS,

MAY WE, YOUR CHILDREN,

DO ALL KINDS OF GOOD THINGS,

IN ALL KINDS OF WONDERFUL WAYS,

IN PLACES FAR AND NEAR,

IN THE MORNING, AT NOON, AND AT NIGHT,

TO ALL KINDS OF PEOPLE,

TODAY, TOMORROW, AND FOREVER.

—INSPIRED BY A
CHARLES WESLEY POEM

MAY TOGETHERNESS OF THIS EARTH
CONTINUE TO GUIDE US,
AND MAY THE DIVINE BRING PEACE
AND UNDERSTANDING
TO PROTECT THE WORLD.

—NIGERIAN BLESSING

REFLECT ON YOUR
PRESENT BLESSINGS,
OF WHICH EVERY MAN HAS MANY;
NOT ON YOUR PAST MISFORTUNES,
OF WHICH ALL MEN HAVE SOME.

—CHARLES DICKENS

MAY THE EARTH
CONTINUE TO LIVE,

MAY THE HEAVENS ABOVE
CONTINUE TO LIVE,

MAY THE RAINS
CONTINUE TO DAMPEN THE LAND,

MAY THE WET FORESTS
CONTINUE TO GROW.

THEN THE FLOWERS SHALL BLOOM
AND WE PEOPLE SHALL LIVE AGAIN.

—HAWAIIAN BLESSING

MAY YOU GO OUT IN JOY
AND BE LED FORTH IN PEACE;

MAY THE MOUNTAINS AND HILLS
BURST INTO SONG BEFORE YOU,

AND ALL THE TREES OF THE FIELD
CLAP THEIR HANDS.

INSTEAD OF THE THORNBUSH,
MAY JUNIPER GROW,

AND INSTEAD OF BRIERS,
MAY MYRTLE GROW.

THIS WILL BE FOR THE LORD'S RENOWN,
AN EVERLASTING SIGN THAT WILL
ENDURE FOREVER.

—INSPIRED BY ISAIAH 55:12-13

MAY GOD WHO IS LIGHT
SHINE IN YOUR DARKNESS.
MAY GOD WHO IS LOVE
BE THE LOVE BETWEEN YOU.
MAY GOD WHO IS LIFE
BE YOUR LIFE EVERLASTING.

—AUTHOR UNKNOWN

IF YOU DO NOT EXPECT,
YOU WILL NOT HAVE.
GOD WILL NOT HEAR YOU
UNLESS YOU BELIEVE
HE WILL HEAR YOU;
BUT IF YOU BELIEVE HE WILL,
HE WILL BE AS GOOD AS YOUR FAITH.

—CHARLES SPURGEON

O GOD, **CREATOR** OF OUR LAND,

OUR EARTH, THE TREES,
THE ANIMALS AND HUMANS,

ALL IS FOR YOUR HONOR.

THE DRUMS BEAT IT OUT,
AND PEOPLE SING ABOUT IT,

AND THEY DANCE WITH NOISY JOY THAT
YOU ARE THE LORD.

—WEST AFRICAN BLESSING

LOOKING BEHIND,
I AM FILLED WITH GRATITUDE.

LOOKING FORWARD,
I AM FILLED WITH VISION.

LOOKING UPWARDS,
I AM FILLED WITH STRENGTH.

LOOKING WITHIN,
I DISCOVER PEACE.

—QUERO APACHE PRAYER

BE PRESENT AT OUR TABLE, LORD,

BE HERE AND EVERYWHERE ADORED.

THY CREATURES BLESS, AND GRANT THAT WE

MAY FEAST IN PARADISE WITH THEE.

—JOHN WESLEY

PARDON, O LORD,
THE IMPERFECTIONS OF
THESE OUR PRAYERS,
AND ACCEPT THEM
THROUGH THE MEDIATION
OF OUR BLESSED SAVIOR.

—JANE AUSTEN

THANK YOU

FOR THE WIND AND RAIN
AND SUN AND PLEASANT WEATHER.
THANK YOU FOR THIS, OUR FOOD,
AND THAT WE ARE TOGETHER.

—MENNONITE TABLE BLESSING

PRAYER IS THE NEAREST APPROACH TO GOD.

—WILLIAM LAW

THE WORDS WE USE
ARE THE WORLDS WE LIVE IN.

—RICHARD FORD

MAY THE BLESSING OF GOD
NOT BRING TO US SAINTS ALONE,
BUT MAKE US SAINTS
GREATER THAN ANY WE IMAGINE.

—DANIEL J. MCGILL

DEAR GOD OF PEACE AND REST
AND COMFORT,

PLEASE BLESS US, YOUR CHILDREN,
FROM HEAD TO TOE.

MAKE US HOLY IN MIND, BODY,
AND SOUL.

YOU HAVE CHOSEN YOUR
CHILDREN, AND YOU ARE FAITHFUL
AND GOOD TO THEM.

FOR THIS, WE THANK YOU AND
PRAISE YOU.

—INSPIRED BY
1 THESSALONIANS 5:23-25

A CHILD'S BEDTIME PRAYER

NOW I LAY ME
DOWN TO SLEEP,

I PRAY THE LORD
MY SOUL TO KEEP:

MAY GOD GUARD ME
THROUGH THE NIGHT

AND WAKE ME WITH
THE MORNING LIGHT.

AMEN.

LORD, SOMEHOW, SOME WAY,
MAKE ME A BLESSING
TO SOMEONE TODAY.
AMEN.

WE SHOULD CERTAINLY
COUNT OUR BLESSINGS,
BUT WE SHOULD ALSO
MAKE OUR BLESSINGS COUNT.

—NEIL A. MAXWELL

MAY THE ROAD

RISE UP TO MEET YOU.

MAY THE WIND BE

ALWAYS AT YOUR BACK.

MAY THE SUN SHINE WARM

UPON YOUR FACE;

THE RAINS FALL SOFT

UPON YOUR FIELDS,

AND UNTIL WE MEET AGAIN,

MAY GOD HOLD YOU

IN THE PALM OF HIS HAND.

—TRADITIONAL GAELIC BLESSING

THANK

GRATITUDE
IS THE KEY TO
HAPPINESS.

— C.S. LEWIS

DEAR LORD,
THANK YOU.

· · · · · · · · · ❧ · · · · · · · · · ·

WHEN YOU PRAY,

MOVE YOUR FEET.

—AFRICAN PROVERB

LORD, I RISE IN THE MORNING,

AND GIVE **THANKS** FOR THE LIGHT.

I GIVE **THANKS**

FOR LIFE, FOR STRENGTH.

I GIVE **THANKS** FOR FOOD

AND FOR THE JOY OF LIVING.

IF EVER I SEE NO REASON

TO GIVE **THANKS**,

THE FAULT LIES IN ME.

—INSPIRED BY TECUMSEH

FOR FLOWERS THAT BLOOM
ABOUT OUR FEET,

FATHER, WE THANK YOU.

FOR TENDER GRASS SO
FRESH AND SWEET,

FATHER, WE THANK YOU.

FOR THE SONG OF BIRD
AND HUM OF BEE,
FOR THE GLORY WE WILL
SOMEDAY SEE,

FATHER IN HEAVEN,
WE THANK YOU.

—INSPIRED BY
RALPH WALDO EMERSON

THE LORD IS NEAR

TO ALL

WHO CALL ON HIM,

TO ALL

WHO CALL ON HIM

IN TRUTH.

—PSALM 145:18

DEAR LORD,

WHO GIVES US LIFE,

PLEASE GIVE US, EVERY DAY,

HEARTS FULL OF

THANKFULNESS

FOR ALL YOU

HAVE GIVEN US!

—INSPIRED BY
WILLIAM SHAKESPEARE

O LORD MY GOD...

THANK YOU FOR GIVING ME
REST IN BODY AND SOUL.
YOUR HAND HAS BEEN OVER ME
AND HAS GUARDED AND PRESERVED ME...
O GOD, YOUR HOLY NAME BE PRAISED.

—DIETRICH BONHOEFFER

YOUR BOUNTY IS BEYOND MY SPEAKING.
BUT THOUGH MY MOUTH BE DUMB,
MY HEART SHALL THANK YOU.

—NICHOLAS ROWE

THANK YOU, LORD JESUS,

THAT YOU WILL BE

OUR HIDING PLACE,

WHATEVER HAPPENS.

—CORRIE TEN BOOM

TO BE A CHRISTIAN WITHOUT PRAYER IS NO MORE POSSIBLE THAN TO BE ALIVE WITHOUT BREATHING.

—MARTIN LUTHER

WE BLESS THEE,
O MOST HIGH GOD
AND LORD OF MERCY,
WHO EVER DOEST WITH US
THINGS BOTH GREAT
AND INSCRUTABLE.

—SAINT BASIL THE GREAT

YOU WILL CALL ON ME AND
COME AND PRAY TO ME,
AND I WILL LISTEN TO YOU.

—JEREMIAH 29:12

LORD, WE **THANK YOU**
FOR YOUR CHURCH,
FOUNDED UPON YOUR WORD,
THAT CHALLENGES US TO DO MORE
THAN SING AND PRAY,
BUT GO OUT AND WORK.

—MARTIN LUTHER KING JR.

THE PEOPLE WHO KNOW GOD WELL—
MYSTICS, HERMITS, PRAYERFUL PEOPLE,
THOSE WHO RISK EVERYTHING TO FIND GOD—
ALWAYS MEET A LOVER, NOT A DICTATOR.

—RICHARD ROHR

> LORD, BECAUSE YOU HAVE ME,
> I OWE YOU THE WHOLE OF MY LOVE;
> BECAUSE YOU HAVE REDEEMED ME,
> I OWE YOU THE WHOLE OF MYSELF.
>
> —SAINT ANSELM

BE NOT FORGETFUL OF PRAYER.
EVERY TIME YOU PRAY,
IF YOUR PRAYER IS SINCERE,
THERE WILL BE NEW FEELING
AND NEW MEANING IN IT,
WHICH WILL GIVE YOU FRESH COURAGE,
AND YOU WILL UNDERSTAND THAT
PRAYER IS AN EDUCATION.

—FYODOR DOSTOEVSKY

DEAR GOD,

PLEASE SURROUND

THE WORLD'S CHILDREN

WITH PEOPLE WHOSE HEARTS

ARE FULL OF LOVE.

MAY THEIR LOVE

REFLECT *YOUR* LOVE,

THE GREATEST LOVE OF ALL.

THANK YOU FOR YOUR LOVE!

FATHER AND PROTECTOR,
I THANK YOU THAT UNDER YOUR WINGS
I CAN ALWAYS FIND REFUGE.

—INSPIRED BY PSALM 91:1

DO NOT BE ANXIOUS
ABOUT ANYTHING,
BUT IN EVERY SITUATION,
BY PRAYER AND PETITION,
WITH THANKSGIVING,
PRESENT YOUR REQUESTS TO GOD.
AND THE PEACE OF GOD,
WHICH TRANSCENDS ALL
UNDERSTANDING, WILL GUARD YOUR
HEARTS AND YOUR MINDS
IN CHRIST JESUS.

—PHILIPPIANS 4:6-7

LORD, WE OFFER YOU THANKS AND PRAISE

FOR THE GIFT OF ALL OUR DAYS.

FOR ALL YOUR GIFTS, OF EVERY KIND

WE OFFER PRAISE, WITH HEART AND MIND.

BE WITH ME, LORD, AND GUIDE MY WAYS

THROUGH ALL MY NIGHTS,

THROUGH ALL MY DAYS.

—INSPIRED BY
  SAINT FRANCIS OF ASSISI

DEAR GOD,

HERE I AM,

THANKING YOU
FOR THE GIFT
OF A NEW DAY.
AMEN.

I LIVE AND BREATHE GOD.

—PSALM 34:2 MSG

LORD, WHEN I FEEL
THAT WHAT I'M DOING IS
INSIGNIFICANT AND UNIMPORTANT,
HELP ME TO REMEMBER
THAT EVERYTHING I DO IS
SIGNIFICANT AND IMPORTANT
IN YOUR EYES,
BECAUSE YOU LOVE ME
AND YOU PUT ME HERE,
AND NO ONE ELSE CAN DO
WHAT I AM DOING
IN EXACTLY THE WAY I DO IT.

—BRENNAN MANNING

ANYTHING IS A BLESSING WHICH
MAKES US PRAY.

—CHARLES SPURGEON

HEAVENLY FATHER,

THANK YOU FOR

CREATING THIS DAY!

NOW, LET'S SEE

WHAT WE CAN

CREATE TOGETHER...

DEAR LORD,

I THANK YOU

FOR EVERY PERSON

WHO WOKE UP

THIS MORNING

DETERMINED TO

MAKE OUR WORLD

A BETTER PLACE.

AMEN.

TODAY, PLEASE GENTLY
REMIND ME THAT YOU ARE
THE FATHER AND I AM THE CHILD.
MAY I BE HUMBLE ENOUGH
TO LEARN FROM YOU.
I THANK YOU FOR
THE GIFT OF HUMILITY.
AMEN.

———

WITH THE GRACE
OF PRAYER,
WE SHALL PREVAIL.

—LAILAH GIFTY AKITA

FOR REST AND SHELTER

THROUGH THE NIGHT,

FOR THE NEXT MORNING

AT ITS LIGHT,

FOR HEALTH AND FOOD,

FOR LOVE AND FRIENDS,

FOR EVERY GIFT THE FATHER SENDS,

WE THANK YOU,

GRACIOUS LORD.

GRATITUDE BEFORE ME,

GRATITUDE BEHIND ME,

GRATITUDE TO THE LEFT OF ME,

GRATITUDE TO THE RIGHT OF ME,

GRATITUDE ABOVE ME,

GRATITUDE BELOW ME,

GRATITUDE WITHIN ME,

GRATITUDE ALL AROUND ME.

—ANGELES ARRIEN

FATHER,

WE CALL THEE FATHER

BECAUSE WE LOVE THEE.

WE ARE GLAD TO BE CALLED

THY CHILDREN,

AND TO DEDICATE OUR LIVES TO THE...

BETTERMENT OF ALL MANKIND.

WE SEND A CRY OF THANKSGIVING

FOR PEOPLE OF ALL RACES,

CREEDS, CLASSES, AND COLORS

THE WORLD OVER.

—MARY MCLEOD BETHUNE
(EXCERPTED FROM BETHUNE'S "SYMPHONY OF LIFE")

THE CROSS IS THE

HOPE OF CHRISTIANS,

THE CROSS IS THE

RESURRECTION OF THE DEAD,

THE CROSS IS THE

WAY OF THE LOST,

THE CROSS IS THE

SAVIOR OF THE LOST.

WE THANK YOU, FATHER,

FOR THE CROSS.

—AFRICAN HYMN

SPEAK, LORD, FOR WE LONG TO HEAR YOU,

SPEAK PEACE TO OUR ANXIOUS SOULS,

AND HELP US TO FEEL THAT ALL OUR WAYS

ARE UNDER YOUR WISE CONTROL;

THAT YOU WHO CARE FOR THE LILY,

AND HEED THE SPARROWS' FALL,

SHALL GENTLY LEAD YOUR LITTLE ONES:

FOR YOU MADE AND LOVE THEM ALL.

—AUTHOR UNKNOWN

SHOW ME YOUR WAYS, Lord,

TEACH ME YOUR PATHS.

GUIDE ME IN YOUR TRUTH AND TEACH ME,

FOR YOU ARE GOD MY SAVIOR,

AND MY HOPE IS IN YOU ALL DAY LONG.

—PSALM 25:4-5

THE SACRED THREE

MY FORTRESS BE

ENCIRCLING ME

COME AND BE ROUND

MY HEARTH AND MY HOME

—CELTIC PRAYER

I THANK YOU TODAY
AND EVERY DAY THAT
YOUR MERCY
TRIUMPHS OVER
JUDGMENT.

———

GOD IS FAITHFUL STILL
AND HEARS PRAYERS STILL.

—GEORGE MÜLLER

MY GENEROUS LORD,

THANK YOU FOR THE ABILITIES AND

RESOURCES YOU HAVE GIVEN ME.

HELP ME TO LIVE A GENEROUS LIFE,

TO SHARE WHAT I HAVE.

LET ME LIVE EVERY DAY

WITH A GRATEFUL HEART.

AMEN.

DEAR GOD,
INTO YOUR HANDS,
I GRATEFULLY
COMMIT MY SPIRIT.

—INSPIRED BY PSALM 31:5

DEAR GOD,
I AM GRATEFUL
THAT WHEN I'M AFRAID
I CAN TRUST IN YOU.
AMEN.

THE CHRISTIAN SHOULD WORK

AS IF ALL DEPENDED UPON HIM, AND

PRAY AS IF IT ALL DEPENDED UPON GOD.

— CHARLES SPURGEON

HOLY GOD,

MAY I HONOR AND

THANK YOU TODAY

BY SLOWING DOWN

AND APPRECIATING

THE BEAUTY

ALL AROUND ME.

GOD, YOU'RE SUCH A

SAFE AND POWERFUL PLACE

TO FIND REFUGE!

YOU'RE A PROVEN HELP

IN TIME OF TROUBLE—

MORE THAN ENOUGH

AND ALWAYS AVAILABLE

WHENEVER I NEED YOU.

—PSALM 46:1 TPT

PRAISE BE TO YOU, LORD;

TEACH ME YOUR DECREES.

—PSALM 119:12

———

PRAYER MAKES A GODLY MAN,
AND PUTS WITHIN HIM THE MIND
OF CHRIST, THE MIND OF HUMILITY,
OF SELF-SURRENDER, OF SERVICE,
OF PITY, AND OF PRAYER.
IF WE REALLY PRAY, WE WILL
BECOME MORE LIKE GOD.

—E.M. BOUNDS

THANK YOU
FOR BEING *FOR* US,
AND NEVER
AGAINST US.

· · · · · · · · · · ❧ · · · · · · · · · ·

EVERY MORNING

LEAN YOUR ARMS AWHILE

UPON THE WINDOWSILL OF HEAVEN

AND GAZE UPON THE LORD.

THEN WITH THE VISION IN YOUR HEART,

TURN STRONG TO MEET YOUR DAY.

—THOMAS BLAKE

I LIFT UP MY EYES

TO THE MOUNTAINS—

WHERE DOES MY
HELP COME FROM?

MY HELP COMES

FROM THE LORD,

THE MAKER OF

HEAVEN AND EARTH.

—PSALM 121:1-2

MY LOVING CREATOR,

THANK YOU FOR CARING

ABOUT MY INMOST BEING.

LET ME NEVER FAIL

TO BE GRATEFUL TO YOU,

FOR I AM FEARFULLY

AND WONDERFULLY MADE.

AMEN.

I THANK YOU THAT TODAY
WILL NOT TAKE ME ANYPLACE
THAT YOUR LOVE AND COMPASSION
CANNOT REACH.

❧

INTO YOUR HANDS

I COMMEND MYSELF,
MY BODY AND SOUL,
AND ALL THINGS.
LET YOUR HOLY ANGEL
BE WITH ME.

—MARTIN LUTHER

GOD, IF THOU DOST NEVER
ANSWER ANOTHER PRAYER
WHILE I LIVE ON THIS EARTH,
I WILL STILL WORSHIP THEE
AS LONG AS I LIVE
AND IN THE AGES TO COME
FOR WHAT THOU HAST
DONE ALREADY.

—A.W. TOZER

"THOUGH THE MOUNTAINS BE SHAKEN
AND THE HILLS BE REMOVED,
YET MY UNFAILING LOVE
FOR YOU WILL NOT BE SHAKEN NOR
MY COVENANT OF PEACE BE REMOVED,"
SAYS THE LORD, WHO HAS
COMPASSION ON YOU.

—ISAIAH 54:10

TODAY I THANK YOU FOR BEAUTY.

I PRAISE YOU

FOR THE WAY THE HEAVENS

DECLARE YOUR GLORY AND

THE SKY ABOVE ME PROCLAIMS

YOUR HANDIWORK.

AMEN.

THANK YOU, GOD,
FOR PUTTING A **NEW SONG**
IN MY HEART.

· · · · · · · · · · ❧ · · · · · · · · · ·

"THANK YOU" IS THE BEST PRAYER
THAT ANYONE COULD SAY.
I SAY THAT ONE A LOT.
"THANK YOU" EXPRESSES
EXTREME GRATITUDE,
HUMILITY, UNDERSTANDING.

—ALICE WALKER

DEAR LORD,

I WILL WAIT ON YOU.

I WILL HOPE IN YOU.

I WILL BE GRATEFUL TO YOU.

HERE I AM.

—INSPIRED BY ISAIAH 8:17-18